FIRST ~~GRADE,~~ HERE I COME!

NANCY CARLSON

To my first grade friends—
I hope you have fun in first grade, too!

PEARSON

Glenview, Illinois • Boston, Massachusetts • Mesa, Arizona • Shoreview, Minnesota • Upper Saddle River, New Jersey

First Grade, Here I Come! by Nancy Carlson. Copyright © Nancy Carlson. All rights reserved including the right of reproduction in whole or in part in any form. This edition published by arrangement with Viking Children's Books, a division of Penguin Young Readers Group, a member of Penguin Group (USA) Inc.

This version of *First Grade, Here I Come!* published by Pearson.

ISBN-13: 978-0-328-38675-8
ISBN-10: 0-328-38675-8

Printed in United States of America. This publication is protected by copyright and permission should be obtained from the publisher prior to any prohibited reproduction, storage in a retrieval system, or transmission in any form or by any means, electronic, mechanical, photocopying, recording, or likewise. For information regarding permission(s), write to: Pearson School Rights and Permissions, One Lake Street, Upper Saddle River, New Jersey 07458

Pearson and Scott Foresman are trademarks, in the U.S. and/or other countries, of Pearson Education, Inc. or its affiliate(s).

4 5 6 7 8 9 10 V008 17 16 15 14 13 12

The first day of school was over, and when Henry got off the bus, his mother and little brother Pete were waiting for him. "How did you like first grade?" asked his mom.

"I didn't like it because I missed kindergarten," said Henry.
"Tell me all about it," said his mom.

"Well, my teacher isn't at all like my kindergarten teacher Ms. Bradley because . . .

"My first-grade teacher is a Mr.!

"But Mr. McCarthy likes my pet worm. And he even has a cool science corner with plants, bugs, rocks, and a guinea pig named Curly."

"The science corner sounds neat!" said Henry's mom.
"Where do you sit?"
"At my own desk that has my name on it."

"Do you sit near any of your friends?"
"No, I didn't know anyone in my class except Tony and Sydney from kindergarten. But guess what?

"I made a new friend named Oswaldo, and he sits next to me!"

"Oswaldo likes soccer and spiders just like I do."

"He sounds nice. Did you learn anything new today?"
"Yes, we learned some math . . .

". . . some new songs with Ms. Cruse, and a science fact.

"Mr. McCarthy also took us to the library,

and he says soon we'll learn how to read books.
But today I already learned one word. . . .

15

"When I have to go to the bathroom, I look for the door that says B-O-Y-S.

"I also learned that when you open Curly's cage door . . .

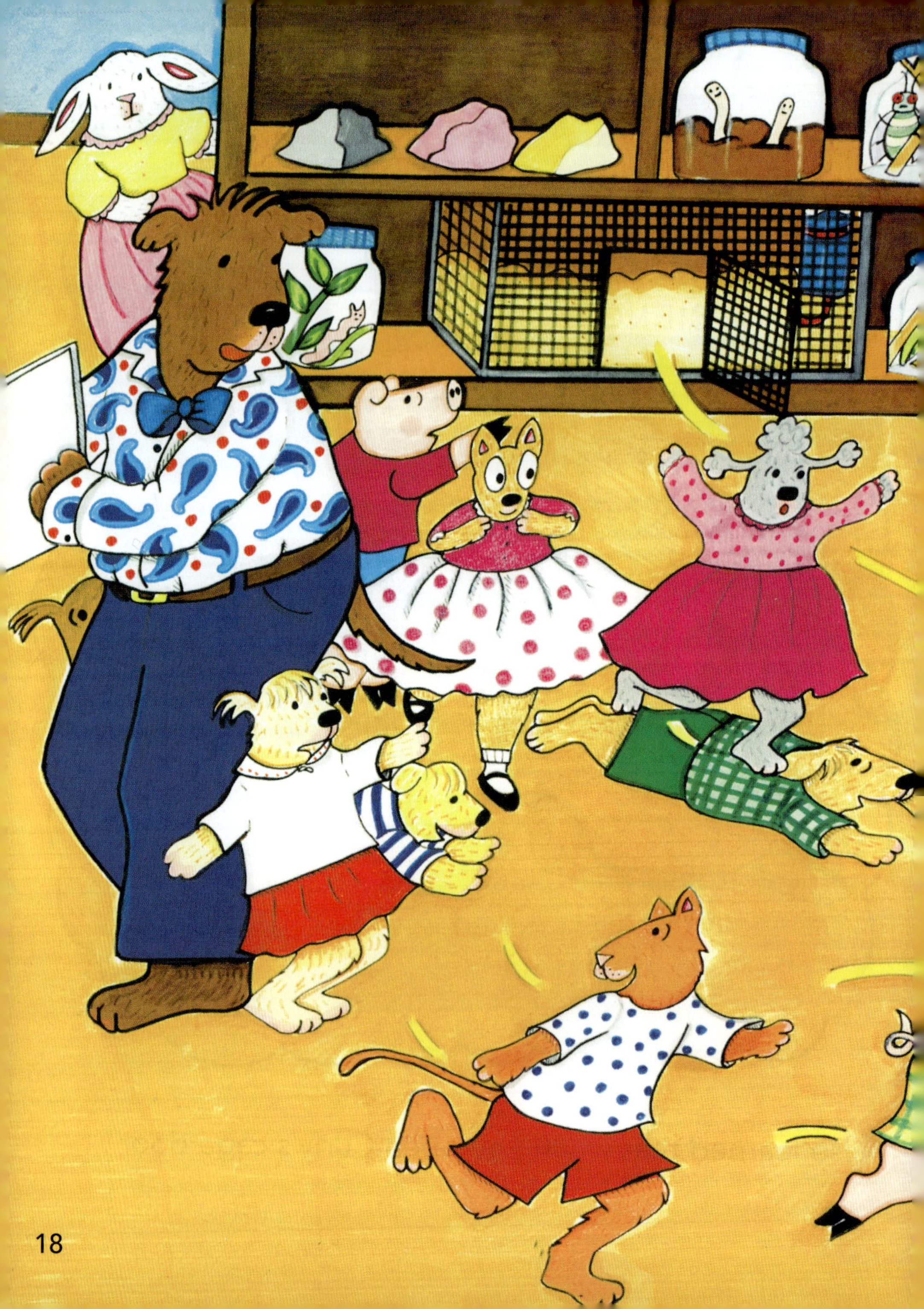

". . . he can run really fast!"

"Wow, you learned a lot! How was lunch?"

"The lunchroom was so big, and I was worried the food would be gross, but . . .

"... tuna melts are really good."

"Did you go out for recess?"
"Yes, but the fifth graders hogged the monkey bars so . . ."

". . . Mr. McCarthy played kickball with us!"

25

"What did you do after recess?" asked his mom.

"We went to art class,

27

"... we had a snack break,

and then I got sent to the principal's office," said Henry.
"Oh, no, did you get in trouble?"

"No, Mr. McCarthy asked me to deliver a note to the principal, and I didn't even get lost."

"Good for you!" said Henry's mom. "First grade does sound different from kindergarten."
"Yeah, but it's not too much for me, because . . .

"I'm a real first grader now!"